STRATEGY OF EARNING MILLIONS OF DOLLARS

The next step towards having six figures in your account.

JANE O. GOLD

By Jane O Gold, copyright 2024. All rights reserved.

This document may not be replicated or reproduced in any form without permission from the publisher. Moreover, the information inside cannot be transferred, stored electronically, or maintained in a database.
The document cannot be copied, scanned, fixed, or kept in its entirety without the publisher's or creator's consent.

TABLE OF CONTENTS

INTRODUCTION 4
ARE RICHES REALLY WHAT YOU DESIRE? 4
CHAPTER ONE 5
THE NEED FOR MONEY 5
CHAPTER TWO 10
THE RIGHT MINDSET 10
    FEAR 13
CHAPTER THREE 15
PRIORITIZE YOURSELF AND SAVE MUCH 15
CHAPTER FOUR 20
GO PRACTICAL AND SET SHORT-TERM GOALS 20
CHAPTER FIVE 24
MAKE A BUDGET. 24
CHAPTER SIX 29
SMART INVESTMENT STEPS TO ACHIEVE YOUR FINANCIAL GOALS. 29
CHAPTER SEVEN 36
FORM SUITABLE FINANCIAL HABITS 36
    CREATE THE HABIT OF READING MORE. 37
    HEALTHY DIETING 39
    NETWORK AND REGULAR VOLUNTEERING 41
    WORK TO IMPROVE YOURSELF 42
    ONLY ACCEPT MEASURED RISKS. 43
    MONITOR YOUR DEVELOPMENT. 44
    PAY ATTENTION WELL. 47
    MAINTAIN PRODUCTIVE COMPANIONSHIP. 47
    REMAIN PERSISTENT. 48
    APPLY FOR A MENTOR. 51
    DON'T PLACE RESTRICTIONS ON YOURSELF. 52

INTRODUCTION
ARE RICHES REALLY WHAT YOU DESIRE?

Although most people claim to want to be affluent, very few actually take the necessary actions to achieve their goals. Contrary to popular belief, becoming wealthy has more to do with other aspects than just having a high paying profession and making smart investments. We can refer to these as the distinctive behaviors of affluent individuals. Self-made millionaires who have amassed and sustained wealth over time share these crucial behaviors.
It is crucial to keep in mind that accumulating wealth is a gradual process. Building riches requires time and work.

If you're ready to work for it, rich habits like the ones we'll cover in this book will help you get there.

The good news is that anybody may start using these behaviors and witness a favorable shift in their financial circumstances.

CHAPTER ONE
THE NEED FOR MONEY

To each person, being wealthy and amassing wealth will mean something different. All that certain person may want is a reasonable wage and a reasonably big house. There are those who aspire to be billionaires and millionaires. What do you want, is the question?

Why is someone a millionaire? A person with a net worth of $1 million or more is considered a millionaire. A straightforward math method based on your net worth is used. You are considered to be a millionaire when the total of your assets and obligations is greater than one million dollars or one million in the currency of your nation.
And that's it!

Being a billionaire is not something that just happens, you have to work hard and have plans in place to make your goals come true. Make sure this is something you desire and wish for yourself.

Many people view money as a method of attaining their objectives and dreams as well as a source of security. It can be used to cover both needs like food, housing, and medical expenses as well as extravagance like luxury automobiles and trips. Others view money as a means of achieving respect, position, and influence in society. Not everyone aspires to be wealthy. A great deal of folks is content to just get by. They are content as long as they have food on the table and enough cash to get by.

A millionaire is not something that you become suddenly wealthy. Yes, you do get that in a select few cases. A person might win the lottery or inherit an old fortune. You still need to understand how to protect your wealth even in these situations. If not, you would quickly lose everything. Regardless of how you became wealthy, you must
still have the desire to stay wealthy. It must be loved by you. And you need to keep it going.

You won't work for something if you don't enjoy it. You refuse to put in the required effort and make the appropriate sacrifices.

Starting to save is one of the quickest paths to becoming a billionaire or millionaire. Develop the habit of saving. Save at least 15% of your income.

Make the maximum annual contribution to your retirement fund.

Steer clear of debt and unnecessary spending in favor of investing to increase your income.

Refrain from succumbing to Lifestyle creep and make an effort to seek assistance when and when needed. Money acts as a medium of trade between people and things. In addition, it serves as a unit of account and a store of value for other items. Most economies operated on bartering before money was created, in which people exchanged the products they already owned for the things they needed. It is impossible to get the necessities of life without money. It can be used as a unit of account to determine the value of other items as well as a store of value. Education is significantly impacted by money.

Here are some pointers on how to hit the million or billion-dollar mark.

1. Establish specific objectives and a plan to meet them.
2. Make prudent investments and save money.
3. Don't be scared to take chances.
4. Have tenacity and never give up. 5. Always learn new things and develop.

6. Take lessons from your errors.
7. Show generosity with both cash and time.

The four everyday purposes of money are to live, give, owe, and develop. The next six are as follows: debt relief, lifestyle choices, family obligations, financial independence, giving to charity, and perhaps even launching a business yourself or assisting someone else in doing so.

By purchasing higher-quality food and housing, money can enhance your pleasure and well-being. The ability to work hard, be dedicated, and have passion are all necessary to get this money.
It cannot be over emphasized. Power comes from money. It gives every person on the planet equal possibilities. You can afford a better education and have more employment alternatives if you have money.

Isn't it lovely to want, pray for, and strive for what brings you comfort?

While money cannot buy happiness in its entirety, well-earned money can provide you with security, independence, and the ability to follow your aspirations. This has the potential to greatly increase your happiness. It is crucial to work hard, earn money, and develop saving and investing skills because of this.

CHAPTER TWO
THE RIGHT MINDSET

Possessing the appropriate mindset is crucial to moving forward and realizing your goals.
You have to maintain your optimism despite the circumstances. A study with two individuals in the desert exists. One individual possesses all the necessary survival skills but has a pessimistic outlook, whereas the other lacks survival skills but has a positive outlook. Which one do you believe will make it? It's the one who exudes optimism.
Even though life can be challenging at times, you'll be happier and have a higher chance of success if you can learn to find the good in everything.

It is impossible to achieve your goals, whether they are financial or not, if you have self-doubt from the beginning. The objective is to believe without reservation, not to doubt. Have faith in your ability to get wealthy. Have faith that you can succeed. Even if you can't see how to get there, you should still have faith that it's achievable. Speaking it out is a simpler approach to accomplish this. Talk to yourself aloud about it. I'm able to go. I'll succeed in achieving it. You'll soon start putting your affirmations into practice, and your dreams will soon come true. For this reason, it is crucial that you have confidence in yourself and think positively as much as you can. Acquire the skill of being patient. Don't always move quickly. A well-known saying goes, "There's no rush in life." We frequently make a lot of blunders when we move too quickly. Refrain from thinking negatively. When we think negatively, most of the time, we think too quickly. It is common for us to make errors. We will be able to avoid making many mistakes if we can learn to take our time when performing certain crucial tasks. Remaining perspective is aided by learning to slow down. When you find yourself thinking negatively, pause, inhale deeply, and consider the circumstances. Look for something to divert your attention You could take a stroll to get your head free of everything bad. You'll notice that your thoughts are lighter and your vision is clearer by the end of the walk. The result is that you have to have made some observations or said hello to someone outdoors throughout your stroll. These diversions aided in altering the way one was thinking. Even in the absence of distractions, taking

in the scenery or the outdoors by staring out of the window or binoculars is beneficial.
filling your head with enjoyable ideas. Your phones' amusing videos can be useful. Laugh aloud. It diverts your attention from descending the well. These brief films lift your spirits and demonstrate what happens when your mind is free of negativity.

Practice remaining upbeat in the face of adversity. Have confidence in yourself. Though you can't completely stop thinking bad thoughts, you can stop yourself from focusing on them and letting them rule your mind.

Keep your emotions under check.
Get a Good Start to the Day You don't have to wake up early like wealthiest people do, which is typically about five in the morning. It is necessary for you to begin your day in the correct manner.

When it comes to making personal financial decisions, emotions can have a big impact. Fear, greed, happiness and anxiety are just a few of the emotions that impact many financial decisions.

Financial decisions might be made irrationally by those who are afraid. When we say anything while

we're feeling very emotional, most of us end up in difficulty. You may think of a couple similar occasions if you take five minutes right now. Consider things carefully and take a step back before speaking your views.
It's likely that you'll be glad you held your tongue.

WHY DOES IT MATTER HOW YOU EXPRESS THINGS?

When it comes to making financial decisions, emotions are a major factor that can either positively or negatively impact the results. Making more logical and advantageous financial decisions is possible if we comprehend behavioral finance and are conscious of our emotions and prejudices. You never know what might turn around and bite you. That is all there is to it.
Therefore, you would be better off biting your tongue even though you might want to tell your boss—who is letting you go—where to stick it. You never know when a reference could come in handy for a future career.

FEAR is the feeling that divides the rich from the poor.

Rich people learn to embrace their fears and grow into confident individuals. They have the bravery to keep going on because of this confidence.

The impoverished, on the other hand, never develop confidence and always give in to dread.

As a result, they become mired in their predicament and never get better.

CHAPTER THREE
PRIORITIZE YOURSELF AND SAVE MUCH

Paying oneself first is a tactic used by both the government and affluent individuals to amass more wealth. It's the easiest path to financial success. You are effortlessly accumulating wealth each and every month when you do this. People save money for a variety of reasons, including the fact that it gives them financial freedom and stability and protects them in the event of an unexpected financial crisis. If one has saved enough money (which varies from person to person), they can pay off debt, live the life of their dreams, and avoid taking on more debt.

You will genuinely start saving money, which will have a great effect on your finances, therefore it's imperative that you pay yourself first even if you aren't saving any. All the knowledge you need to improve your financial condition is available here. Let's think about this for a minute. Examine your life as it is right now. If you keep making and spending the same amount of money, how much money will you have in ten years? In the long run, your financial situation will deteriorate if you continue to live beyond your means. Every month will bring with it more debt, anxiety, and headaches as you wonder how you're going to make ends meet.

You will still be barely surviving in ten years if you are struggling to make ends meet now.

In the end, if you aren't saving anything, you won't be wealthy or even be able to escape the cycle of earning and spending.

However, your financial situation will alter if you do begin saving money. When crises arise, you will be financially secure. With your money, you can live a better life. And one day you'll have enough money to retire.

ARE YOU STILL UNSURE ABOUT HOW PAYING YOURSELF FIRST WILL FUNCTION?

Based on the incomes from the previous years, taxes were initially mailed to the government. Yet, the government eventually found that most people save little to nothing, put money aside later, and then run out of money before they can pay their taxes. Then the government began paying its own bills first. It was an easy fix. Before you are paid, it deducts their money from your paycheck. This ensures they will always receive their money.

Companies that offer mutual funds work in the same way. You will undoubtedly accumulate wealth if you put yourself first. You must instantly begin saving money. Furthermore, a large sum of money is not necessary. Prior to making any purchases, save aside a tiny portion of your paycheck each time you get paid.

The majority of people claim to want to be wealthy, but very few actually do the required actions. Contrary to popular belief, being affluent has more components than just a lucrative career and well-chosen assets. These are what we might refer to as the affluent people's distinguishing habits. These are essential behaviors of self-made millionaires who have amassed and preserved money over time.
It's critical to keep in mind that accumulating wealth takes time.
Getting rich takes time and work. These wealthy habits will help you get there if you're ready to put in the effort. The good news is that everyone can

adopt these routines and observe a favorable improvement in their financial circumstances.

It is important to maintain a balance between your living expenses and income. Additionally, avoid taking on debt to make purchases you cannot afford. There may be an exception for necessities like a home, good health, etc., but not for luxury items. Aim to put aside as much cash as you can for cloudy days. Your financial situation will never improve if you don't save anything.

You can miss out on an opportunity if you haven't saved or made plans for it. In fifteen years, your life now will not change if you do not save. You will be in much worse financial situation in fifteen years if you spend more than you make.

One of the most important components of accumulating wealth and ensuring a stable financial future is saving money. Having savings allows you to escape the unknown.

- It is useful in an emergency.

Emergencies never come as planned.

  - It protects against an unexpected job loss. Even if you might have a great job right now, what would happen if you lost it?

- Assists in providing funding for significant life events and expensive purchases.
- Reduces debt.... • Aids with retirement planning.

Apart from prioritizing financial savings, there are several other actions you can do to reduce the expenses you are now incurring.
For instance, as a student you can renew your student loan debt to save money each month.
You might also consider refinancing this if you have a mortgage.
Refinancing might potentially result in monthly savings of hundreds. Additionally, you should prioritize paying off any credit card debt you may have as soon as feasible. You may start building your savings more quickly than you would have imagined by putting in a little work.

Every month, make it a point to save money. It is impossible to overstate this. For now, don't bother about the sum. Just start saving as a habit right now. A six-month reminder can help you save even more money.
Next, schedule an additional reminder to raise this amount by at least 1% once a year, every year.

CHAPTER FOUR
GO PRACTICAL AND SET SHORT-TERM GOALS

Make wise goals. A goal is something over which you have control over the likelihood of success. You have absolutely no control over a wish. For example, if your aim was to accumulate $5 million, you would create an action plan and take measures to increase your chances of achieving the goal. and would begin monitoring your advancement as well. Your aim might not be achieved. However, that does not mean that everything you did to accomplish the aim was in vain. It's likely that you currently make more money than you did in the past. putting you in a better financial position than you were previously. You would also have developed personally and learnt a lot about yourself.

For example, you could choose to set aside $200,000. You can choose any amount, but we'll choose $200,000 for the purposes of this writing. Yes, that's a large objective. Although it may seem impossible, breaking your large goals down into smaller, more doable tasks will help you stay motivated and increase your chances of success. Though you may not have anything saved at all. You may believe that saving that much amount is unachievable. This is a common way of feeling. But you shouldn't give up. It is claimed that one small step can lead to a mile.

Some people experience this feeling only a few months later. After putting in a lot of effort to save, you notice that you are only a few dollars short of your target. Then you feel depressed and give up because you know it will take a lifetime to get there. No, you shouldn't. Instead, you should divide your ambitious objectives into smaller, more doable tasks.

You'll stay motivated if you do this, and you'll have a higher chance of reaching your intended outcome. For example, rather than setting a goal to save a large sum of money, like $15,000, you may choose to divide it up into smaller goals, like $1500 each month or quarter, based on your income, and recognize your accomplishments when you reach the mark.

Yes, your initial objective was to receive $15,000, but reaching it gradually would help you feel less anxious, stressed, and less desire to punish yourself.

Celebrate your accomplishment once you've raised the first $1500 toward your goal. Enjoy a delicious dinner and a refreshing beverage, stay positive, and make another objective to earn the remaining amounts. Once you've done it, rejoice once more, get fresh motivation, and make new goals. You wouldn't notice right away that you've saved up $15,000. There might be more.

You can pay off your bills with the aid of this method. Don't go overboard, with one small quantity at a time. If you are persistent, you will soon be grinning since you will have easily paid off your debt.

It is more beneficial to concentrate on smaller cash amounts at a time rather than a larger sum. A lesser aim allows you to realize your ambition more quickly. You can set savings targets of $1,000 and observe how much simpler it is to reach those amounts. Once your smaller objective has been accomplished, celebrate and set a new one. Don't stop moving; keep going. Investing pre-tax money is an additional method of saving money. A retirement plan, which permits you to pay tax when you withdraw at a lower retirement tax rate than your current tax rate, is accessible to many people who work full-time. By making these investments, you also reduce your taxable income and your current tax liability.

Make money-saving simple, you can by automating the procedure, you achieve this. Visit your bank and arrange for a regular deposit into your savings account. Your income and expenses will determine how much money you can save.

The idea is to automate the transfer so that you never have to worry about saving additional money. Let it be an account where you are receiving interest as well. A competitive interest rate must be earned on your rainy-day fund. By doing this, compound interest will enable every dollar you save to increase at a faster rate. This is a fancy way of expressing that you earn interest in addition to the interest payments you receive. Because you are getting larger returns, your money grows more quickly.

You learn that striving to accomplish your objective gradually has improved both your financial situation and your level of personal growth.

CHAPTER FIVE
MAKE A BUDGET.

Make a spending plan. A budget can be as specific as you want it to be. Although it doesn't sound enjoyable, it's not as horrible as you may assume. Learn to set aside money for each and every cost. You can change things so that you only set aside money for bills you found hard to manage, like entertainment and eating out.

For many, the first step to budgeting is overcoming the perception that a budget compels you to lose out on living today for a happy tomorrow. If this describes you, start viewing a budget as a tool to assist you in meeting your savings objectives. Even as you work toward earning your first $100,000, you can still enjoy yourself and have fun.

You might be able to come up with an affordable plan. There are lots of possibilities available. If you want complete control over your spending, you can use a spreadsheet.

You can identify areas where you could be overspending and take appropriate action by tracking where your extra money is going. When you begin budgeting, you'll discover, for example, how much you spend on eating out. A few individuals would dine out many times within a given month. You may not have realized how your finances were affected by the amount you perceive as modest each time. You may believe that $10–$20 is a pitiful amount of money. However, if you added them all up and said you went out to eat five or six times a month, you would discover that you had spent a lot of money.

Budgeting encourages you to question purchases more. You may have thought about buying more before paying, but now you would start to ask yourself whether you need that much. Then you will gradually reduce buying unnecessary items thereby saving more money. When you examine how much each meal would have cost if you had eaten out, packing your meals can occasionally lead you to realize you have saved a significant amount of money in a month.

You would be surprised how much you saved in a year.

Making the transition to a cash-only lifestyle is another choice.

You'll spend less if you pay with cash for everything you purchase. Psychological factors are at play. There's a disconnect when we use a plastic credit card, and we don't think about the price.

However, we consider our purchases carefully before making them when we have cash in our pockets. If you are unable to do this, consider investigating charge cards.

Similar to a credit card, a charge card requires full repayment each month. In the long run, you will save money by avoiding carrying costs over into the following month.

The end objective is to contribute as much as you can to your nest egg each month. However, this does not mean that you have to give up all of your pleasures and live a miserable life. Strike a balance between spending and saving. If you are in debt, it is a red flag. Therefore, you should avoid going into debt at all costs.

The sooner you pay off your bills, the sooner you can take that money and start saving it, which will cause it to increase even further.

Pay off one loan at a time, paying it off as soon as possible.

Putting this into practice will inspire you to keep going.

You decide which debt to pay off next and concentrate on doing it gradually, one payment at a time.

Continue until all of your bills are paid off. Furthermore, saving some of your income is essential, but you can expedite the process by setting aside more. When it comes to increasing your wealth, your career is your best asset.

To begin with, consider your existing position. By going outside, the scope of your work description, you can easily raise your yearly income by 5% or more. Furthermore, there are other areas you can focus on to boost your income outside your pay. Choose a side project to work on in your free time to earn extra money. Additionally, if you choose wisely, you won't feel like you're working. You would be thrilled to carry it out. Recall that you will achieve the magic number faster if you make more money than you can save. It all depends on you and your objectives.

As soon as your side business starts bringing in money, you may want to upgrade your vehicle or go on a lengthy trip.

Try your best to resist this urge.

Everything you earn on the side can go into your nest egg, provided you create a budget, keep your costs modest, and are able to live comfortably on that paycheck.

You can save your first $100,000 more quickly than you might have imagined if you follow along.

Purchasing assets that have the potential to increase in value financially is the aim of investing. A house, for instance, may be a wise financial investment because of its potential for growth.

Invest in real estate, money market funds, stocks, bonds, mutual funds, and exchange-traded funds (ETFs). Investments carry a range of risks in addition to potential financial rewards. Purchasing stocks, for instance, has the potential to increase your wealth over an extended period of time, but there is no assurance that the companies you invest in will prosper.

It's crucial to thoroughly analyze your investments due to risk. You might think about speaking with a financial advisor if you require assistance.

CHAPTER SIX
SMART INVESTMENT STEPS TO ACHIEVE YOUR FINANCIAL GOALS.

These steps can help you achieve your financial objectives more quickly by getting you to six figures and establishing financial security.

First, you have to invest some of your extra cash in order to get there. Second, determine how much risk you can tolerate.
It's crucial to get this right because if you sell when the market drops and you take on too much risk, you will lose more money.
To achieve your goal, just enough risk must be taken. Too much greed will cause you to lose everything. Determining your risk tolerance can be done in a variety of ways.
A 60/40 portfolio is a fantastic choice for many individuals. You invest 40% in bonds and 60% in stocks or shares. The simplest portfolio is 40% invested in the entire bond market and 60% in an exchange-traded fund (ETF) or mutual fund that tracks the S&P 500 Index.

Selecting an investment location is the last stage. You must set yourself up as though you were embarking on a lengthy journey because successful investment is a journey rather than an event. The most prosperous investors did not become wealthy overnight. It takes time and patience to learn the ins and outs of the financial world and your personality as an investor, not to mention trial and error.

Have a goal and timeline before you begin investing. Once you know what you intend to gain and how long you plan to invest for, you can put the necessary structures in place to make it happen. Discover what kind of investor you are, what investment plan is best for you, and how the market functions. As you choose the best course of action for yourself, use caution in the people you listen to and be aware of any biases or preconceptions you may have. Recognize that this is a long-term adventure in order to avoid being sidetracked by temporary setbacks; remain open-minded and constantly willing to learn from your errors. You must set yourself up for success as though you were embarking on a lengthy journey because successful investment is a journey rather than a one-time event.

Set your goals first, and then organize your financial journey accordingly. For instance, do you intend to retire at age 55 in 20 years? How much cash are you going to need for this? These are the things you have to ask first. Your investing goals will determine the plan you develop.

Examine literature or enroll in a course on investments that covers contemporary financial concepts. It is for good reason that those who developed theories like market efficiency, diversification, and portfolio optimization were awarded Nobel awards. A blend of science (fundamentals of finance) and art (qualitative aspects) goes into investing.

You may create straightforward guidelines that work for you after you understand what the market will bear. **"Never invest in a business you cannot understand."** An individualist, or someone who demonstrates analytical behavior, confidence, and a keen sense of worth, typically achieves the best financial results. If, on the other hand, you find that you have more of an adventurous nature, you can still succeed in investing provided you modify your approach accordingly.

Watch out for phony allies who merely pose as being in your corner, like some dishonest financial advisors whose goals might not coincide with yours. It's also important to keep in mind that big financial institutions are your rivals as an investor.
They have larger resources, such as quicker and more extensive access to information.

Remember that you could be your own worst adversary. You can be undermining your own success, depending on your approach, disposition, and specific situation. Large losses that can come from high-risk, high-return investments would affect you significantly more because you are a wealth preserver and risk adverse.

Recognize and address the things that are keeping you from investing profitably or pushing you beyond your comfort zone. Be honest with yourself. When it comes to accumulating wealth, you could be your own worst adversary. You could spot something expensive and decide to buy it instead of saving it for a rainy day, or you become afraid when the market turns shaky. Consider your demons carefully and make an effort to vanquish them. If it's excessive spending, give up buying when you're bored and engage in other activities. Learn about how it functions. Over time, you will do better if you can control your weakness to a greater extent.

Choose the Proper Investment Course. The direction you take should be determined by your personality, resources, and level of understanding. Investors typically use one of the following approaches:

    Avoid putting every one of your eggs in one basket. Your keyword should be "diversity. "You may also place all of your eggs in one basket, but be sure to keep a close eye on it. A core passive portfolio can benefit from tactical bets to combine the two techniques.

The majority of profitable investors begin with diverse, low-risk portfolios and pick up skills over time. Investors are better equipped to adopting a more active role in their portfolios as their knowledge grows over time. Being a successful investor takes time to develop, and the investment process itself is usually drawn out. Occasionally, the market will refute your claims. Recognize that and draw lessons from your errors.

Monitoring your advancement is crucial as it will sustain your motivation while you travel. You won't suddenly become wealthy or achieve six figures in a year, after all. It pays enormous dividends to stay informed about your position. The most effective method for monitoring your advancement is to employ a reliable personal finance formula: Determine your net worth. Your net worth can be calculated by simply deducting your liabilities from your assets. Keep in mind that if you have a lot of debt and little saved, this figure may be negative. Even so, as you pursue your dream of becoming a millionaire, you may still boost your net worth by making wiser decisions. Perhaps you could inquire as to how frequently you should figure out your net worth. It's okay to calculate at the end of the month, but it's better to do so every three months or twice a year.

Establishing a business is a wise investment; self-employed people and entrepreneurs account for three out of every four millionaires. If you're interested in becoming wealthy, you might want to think about starting your own business.

Even so, starting a business is typically not a fast path to financial success because it takes time for a business to expand and become profitable. However, you will succeed if you are persistent, hardworking, and patient. Entrepreneurs who are successful typically possess creativity, flexibility, persistence, and passion.

If you have these qualities, starting your own business could be a smart strategy to increase your wealth.

CHAPTER SEVEN
FORM SUITABLE FINANCIAL HABITS

Rich people manage their money well, which helps them stay wealthy and successful. It is the impoverished who will go bankrupt, not the wealthy who wins the lotto.

This is because those who are wealthy tend to have sound financial practices. They won't use their money to make foolish choices. Most of it is saved and invested, with the remaining portion being spent. These wealthy practices also apply to every aspect of personal finance. They use tax planning strategies to minimize their tax liability.

When they take out loans, they are prudent and only take out what they really need. Additionally, they pay low interest rates because they have excellent credit.

Understand the fundamentals of personal finance and incorporate wealthy people's daily practices. And you'll notice an increase in wealth over time.

CREATE THE HABIT OF READING MORE.

Reading is vital since it sharpens your intellect and provides you with a wealth of information and life lessons.
It improves your comprehension of the environment you live in.
It stimulates your creativity and keeps your mind engaged.
Reading expands your vocabulary and strengthens your ability to communicate.
Numerous prosperous businessmen have acknowledged that reading has contributed to their current success. Reading will help you as an entrepreneur develop your memory for concepts and information. You're expanding creatively and emotionally, and you're thinking in novel ways. These are strong knowledge and skill sets.
Reading introduces you to fresh viewpoints, concepts, and modes of thought. It also enables you to advance your development, enhance your qualities, and quicken your progress. Reading on a regular basis is one of the best habits you can form, even though not everyone has the time or desire to do so.

Strong reading comprehension skills enable workers to follow directions more readily, recognize critical information more quickly, act on it, collaborate more effectively, and spot and fix errors in written materials. Your efforts to enhance yourself will have a ripple effect on other aspects of your life, such as your career and money.

The secret is to read self-improvement literature. The majority of successful people read biographies, current affairs, personal development literature, and career improvement materials. Read those not just to better yourself. Read a variety of books, including self-improvement non-fiction and a good fiction book. Even though you might not think you have the time, you can make reading a regular part of your day. An hour or so before going to bed, turn off the TV and read. Sometimes reading a book is a better option than watching television. You could purchase audio books and listen to them while doing chores, during a lunch break, or on your commute. You are able to. All you need to do is resolve to read. Don't spend too much time on social media. You will benefit more from breaking this behavior as soon as possible. Setting a time limit for yourself on social media is one of the best daily success habits you can form. Work on abstaining for few hours at a time and gradually increase the duration of this interval. Instead, take a walk or pick up a book. You will benefit from improved physical and mental health as a result.

HEALTHY DIETING

Generally speaking, there are two methods to increase your income: working harder or working smarter. Consider your health as well. Eating a better diet can help you achieve both. Eating a better diet will give you more energy and boost your productivity.

It has been discovered that individuals who select healthier meal options consume less overall, which saves money, and are happier with their selections, which saves time. They also discovered that the cost of healthier foods is typically higher than that of junk or comfort food.

The negative effects of inadequate diet on health are widely recognized. However, studies suggest that the negative effects don't end there—it can also be expensive. Even if people choose low-quality foods in an attempt to save money, they may be doing the exact opposite and wind up spending more on medical bills.

According to research, the poor consume the second-highest quantity of junk food. Who eats the most is the middle class.

When the majority of your diet consists of junk food calories and excessive alcohol and soda consumption, your body is not functioning at its best. It is attempting to purge itself of the trash and survive on the tiny amount of nourishment you are giving it. Bad eating impairs concentration and focus, and it depletes your energy levels. You have trouble sleeping, so you wake up exhausted. You are more likely to give in to undesirable habits and make poor decisions when this occurs. However, eating a nutritious diet improves your body's function and your quality of sleep, which gives you more willpower and helps you make wiser decisions. Poor eating habits cause you to wake up exhausted or find it difficult to concentrate. Establish a nutritious eating regimen to improve your performance. Restrict the quantity of junk food you consume.

NETWORK AND REGULAR VOLUNTEERING

Wealthy individuals engage in networking and volunteer work at a rate of over 50%, and 70% donate to charities. This offers the most return. Giving back to the community feels nice.

You may take advantage of opportunities when they arise by volunteering and growing your network. You'll be presented with more opportunities the more individuals you know. These could be work openings or even the chance to attend conferences and other gatherings where you can interact with others who share your interests. When you network, you can even come across new clients or consumers. You are more likely to take advantage of an opportunity when you are joyful and in a good mood than when you are not.

If you speak with successful people, they will tell you that their success was mostly due to their preparation. They took actions to position themselves so they could seize opportunities.

WORK TO IMPROVE YOURSELF

Be industrious and productive. Rich people prioritize improving themselves. This entails picking up new talents in addition to aiming for excellent relationships and health.

They will be more effective at business and in relationships the more they work on themselves. There will be spillover effects from this personal growth in other domains.

The wealthy understand that the stock market works in their favor. They require a respectable return on their investment in order to increase their wealth. They then start investing their money after learning the fundamentals. However, assuming they save anything at all, the ordinary person deposits their money into savings accounts. Considering they worked hard to earn their money, they believe this to be a safe investment. The issue lies in the fact that they cannot increase their money through the use of a bank account.

You should still invest even if it terrifies you. Even with cautious investing, you can get a respectable return. Alternatively, you could consider investing in real estate, as it typically has less volatile prices than the stock market.

Building wealth through rental property ownership is a terrific idea. You will have less financial hardships and be in better shape even if you only make 5% on your investment.

In the end, investing your money allows you to increase your wealth and create opportunities for a brighter future.

ONLY ACCEPT MEASURED RISKS.

Life is full of risks, but only take calculated ones. Certain risks are foolish.

Wealthy people typically take safer, more measured risks. They carefully consider the advantages and disadvantages and determine whether taking a risk is worthwhile before acting.

If so, they accept the chance and are content with the result, even if it means losing money. If something goes wrong, they try to figure out where it went wrong and fix it.

It indicates that they are open to the risk of failing. <u>weigh the benefits and drawbacks before taking any action. your life will improve as a whole the more you do this since you will make fewer mistakes overall. consider long-term impact</u>

Before taking any action, consider how things will affect the long run. Your situation will improve the more of this you can accomplish.

Your ability to succeed financially is greatly influenced by your thought process. Examine the big picture and draw valid comparisons. Additionally, be sure to consider the long-term advantages.

All too often, individuals consider the long-term benefit—which is typically far larger than the initial cost—while focusing only on the upfront expense and deciding something isn't worth it.

MONITOR YOUR DEVELOPMENT.

It's critical to monitor your development. Keeping track of your progress enables you to identify areas for improvement and areas where adjustments are needed. Among the most underappreciated habits of the wealthy is this one. In order to continue doing what is effective and cease doing what is not, they make it a point to track their progress. Monitoring one's net worth is the most straightforward method for individuals to benefit from this.

This is an easy habit that will make a big difference in your future financial situation.

Make a list of all of your liquid assets and debts, then deduct your liabilities—also known as debts—from your assets. That figure is your net worth. The better, the higher the number.

This test measures your ability to save and accumulate wealth. Additionally, calculating it on a daily basis will help you develop the proper mentality so that you can make wise financial decisions and eventually increase your net worth. Make it your mission to determine your net worth on a regular basis and refrain from putting it off.

For some people, procrastination is a major problem. You have tasks to complete, yet you keep putting them off and squandering time. Something crucial that you must accomplish; otherwise, you will never improve. Nothing will change in the slightest.

Act quickly and adhere to your goals if you have any. To get over putting things off; here are tips to help you.

- Make a list of tasks.

- Minimize the amount of decisions you have to make all day. Concentrate on a realistic goal.
Modify your surroundings;
- Assign a companion

Making a to-do list helps you stay organized, stay motivated as you check tasks off the list, and stay aware of what has to be done.

Sort your list in order of priority. Assign the highest priority to the items that will have the most effects, and the lowest priority to the items with the least effects.

Find a partner to hold accountable for assisting you in achieving your objective in addition to creating a list. This might be your partner, a member of your family, or even a friend. You will probably accomplish your goals if you have someone to support you in staying on track, encourage you when things become hard, and rejoice with you when you get there. You can significantly reduce your likelihood of procrastinating by having an outside influence.

PAY ATTENTION WELL.

Resolve to speak less and listen more. It's one of the secrets to being rich. Simply listening to people speak can teach you a great deal.

In social settings, it is sometimes easy to identify the wealthy individual since they tend to listen more than they speak.

It is possible to learn how not to approach an issue instead of how to solve one. Listening to others can teach you a lot, including strategies they employ and the steps they took to achieve success.

MAINTAIN PRODUCTIVE COMPANIONSHIP.

Steer clear of toxic people; it may be challenging, particularly if they are relatives, but it's for the best. Your companions reflect who you are. This implies that you will almost certainly turn into a troublemaker yourself if you associate with troublemakers. You should take some time to review all of your relationships and minimize or eliminate those that don't make you or your life better. It can be simple to break up with harmful friends. It's not as easy as it would be if it involved relatives.

You can restrict your time with them even if you might not want to stop seeing them entirely. Remind yourself of all the positive things in your life and the objectives you have set for yourself. This aids in coping with the detrimental effects of your relationships with these individuals. You must go through this procedure if you wish to achieve success and fortune.

We are impacted by external factors, even those in our inner circle. List all the persons in your life, then give each one a rating. Do they help you in a good way or do they hurt you in some way? Increase your time with them if they make a positive difference. Reduce your time spent with them if they are detrimental.

Seek out and get to know successful individuals. You must locate successful people if you don't already know any.

REMAIN PERSISTENT.

We need to start viewing failure more positively and shift the way we think about it. It is inevitable that you will fail on your path to success. Fail because you are attempting something new and developing yourself. Attempting to be the finest version of

yourself will lead to several failures. There will be moments on your path to achievement when you falter and fall, and that's okay. After a short while, consider the reasons for your failure and try again. Remain persistent. Failure is but one more hiccup on the path to achievement. Don't lose heart; instead, reflect on your mistakes, make corrections, and try again. If you can look at what went wrong with objectivity and focus on fixing it, the chances are that you will see results. Put your past behind you and cease viewing failure negatively. Keep in mind that, as long as you take the time to learn from your mistakes, failing is a necessary aspect of personal development. When you don't succeed, identify what went wrong and try again until you do.
A shift in perspective toward failure can lead to significant personal development.

Increase your self-confidence and get rid of self-limiting ideas. Look for the good in every circumstance. You'll be happy the more you can concentrate on the positive. And this joy will spread to other aspects of your life.

Not that you can't see the drawbacks; just try not to focus on them. Experience the shift by adopting more positive thoughts. There are those among us who excel in demeaning oneself. That's incorrect of you to do that. Rather of believing you are incompetent declare, "You are successful." Declare it aloud. I draw success to myself. Declare it out loud to yourself. I'm not that bad. I am not stupid; I am not alone. I AM WITH GOD. Everything has come together for my benefit because of him. The cosmos is supporting me with the aid of God, who is also my shepherd.

I have wealth.

Positive changes are occurring.

I have sufficient intelligence

All in all, adopting an optimistic mindset is the first step toward being wealthy or simply happy. Next, take appropriate action. Your outlook and mood will improve if you try hard to maintain an optimistic attitude and begin convincing yourself that things may change.

You'll get started on the path to accomplishing your objectives.

You wouldn't believe how many poor individuals have become wealthy. How come not you?

APPLY FOR A MENTOR

It really helps to have a companion or partner that inspires you and can assist you in achieving your objectives. If you chase wealth and success mindlessly, it will be considerably more difficult to get either. Find a mentor and establish a relationship with them as a priority.

Anywhere you go, whether it's to work or church, you may find a mentor. Asking friends and family members whether they know of any successful people who would be a good fit for you is another option.

Finding a mentor is similar to striking gold.

Look for and identify successful individuals who have attained the level of achievement you aspire to. Make friends with them and learn from them. You'll be shocked at how willing they are to share knowledge with you that will enable you to succeed. Your chances of success are significantly increased when you have someone on your side who has already accomplished the desired outcome. So, spend some time looking for other accomplished individuals and asking if they would be willing to mentor you.

Get ready for the opportunities that lie ahead. While anyone can predict what opportunities may present themselves, those who are fortunate enough to seize opportunities often find themselves in the right location at the right moment. When the chance arises, they get ready and are prepared.

They maintain good credit and save money, giving them the means to seize opportunities.

They maintain a network and surround themselves with other accomplished individuals in order to be among the first to learn about new ventures and businesses.

DON'T PLACE RESTRICTIONS ON YOURSELF.

Take some time to consider your goals and desires in life. What brings you joy? What motivates you to live each day as you wake up from bed? As soon as you realize this, make plans to make it a reality.

Take actions that bring you joy. You'll achieve greater success. It's likely that you won't give your all if you work a job you detest. This implies that your chances of receiving promotions or a respectable raise are low. Usually, it's advisable to look for work elsewhere.

A job you love is never really work. You like every second of it. It brings you joy to brag about your accomplishments. Finding the things, you enjoy doing and being aware of your abilities are crucial. Next, determine whether you can use your abilities and those activities to make a living. By achieving this, you will greatly increase your chances of success and prosperity

Lastly, start small and go slowly; I understand that implementing all of these suggestions at once can be intimidating. It's not a competition. Your habits are more likely to remain around in the long run if you are more patient with them. Examining these affluent people's behaviors and affluent individuals, and in no time the world will be yours, and the sky will be your limit. You would become extremely successful and opulently wealthy.

Strategy of Earning Millions of Dollars

www.ingramcontent.com/pod-product-compliance
Lightning Source LLC
Chambersburg PA
CBHW070419230526
45471CB00006B/2886